Attention to Detail:
A Look at Walt Disney World Parks

Volume 1

Keith Black ~ Author/Graphics
Jacquelyn Damon ~ CoAuthor/Photographer

Table of Contents

THANK YOU!

This book would not have been
possible without the Lord's blessing
and help of some very special people.

Thanks must be given to Jackie for the hundreds
of photographs she has taken over the years at the Walt Disney
World Parks, without which this book would not have been possible,
and her encouragement and support in this endeavor.

Thanks also to my wife, Angie, and daughters, Kristen and Lauren,
for their help in looking over this book numerous times as well as
making that first trip together to Walt Disney World so memorable.
If it was not for that trip I may never have been introduced to the work
of Walt Disney and his Imagineers.

Introduction

Since first visiting Walt Disney World in Orlando, Florida with my wife and two daughters in 2003, I began to try and figure out what makes the parks so enjoyable that we all can not wait to return to experience and explore them more.

After reading through many websites, books, and forums as well as listening to podcasts on the subject of Disney, I was drawn to Walt Disney and his vision to provide a clean, entertaining place for families to have fun together. Walt also had a constant desire to improve his creation. His attention to detail and design of guest interaction with the parks intrigued me. He combined his skill as a cartoonist with the fields of film making, architecture and engineering to create what he called Imagineering. Using this unique mixture enabled Walt to fulfill his vision and immerse families into a world of fantasy and imagination. I soon realized the amount of research and effort that went into the parks at Walt Disney World and the fact that there is so much design and detail put into each of these parks that many people do not even realize. Even worse they do not get to experience them. People that do realize this fact still admit to not having seen it all.

So, I have joined with Jackie Damon, another Disney detail enthusiast who I met on the Be Our Guest Podcast Forums, to bring awareness to the incredible work that Walt Disney and his Imagineers have put into these Disney parks. We hope to accomplish this using photographs taken by Jackie during her many trips to the Walt Disney World parks in Orlando, Florida. We seek to test your memory of details you may have seen while on your past visits to the parks and encourage you to take the time to explore and find even more in future visits! Throughout the book we will add insight and information that we have gathered along the way from numerous books, websites, tours, and especially Cast Members working at the parks.

We will begin by taking a broad look at details in the parks and then zoom in a little closer with each level. Each level will consist of thirty-three images of details we have selected from each of the four Disney parks in Orlando, Florida: The Magic Kingdom Park, The Animal Kingdom Park, EPCOT and Disney's Hollywood Studios.
The levels will be as follows:

LEVEL 1: The Weenie Level
LEVEL 2: The Prop Level
LEVEL 3: The Pixie Dust Level

Alongside each detail we have added a small notation area for your use. Let's look at the following example:

Detail 000:

Park: *Magic Kingdom*

Area: *Hub*

Location: *the castle as*

viewed from the hub

First, list the park the detail is located in. Next, determine the area it is in. This could be the land, area or section of the park like Fantasyland, Asia, World Showcase or Main Street. Finally, describe the exact location of the detail image.

At the end of each level will be a first and second help in case you get stuck or just want to make sure you are thinking of the right location. The first help will reveal the park location while the second help will give more specifics.

Along the way we will have feature details which will be marked with a flash ✳! These details will contain additional information that we learned about, or noticed, during our visits to the parks at Walt Disney World.

Following the levels will be an Answer Section containing the location of all the Disney park details in this book. Many detail answers will even contain additional information, images and tidbits for you to dwell on.

Also included in this book are a couple of scavenger hunts for you to explore with family and friends on future visits to the parks. So we hope you enjoy this compilation of details while remembering Walt and the Imagineers who created them for you to encounter.

Let's get started and see if you have been paying attention to detail!

Magic Kingdom opened October 1, 1971.
It was to be an improved design from the park in California.
Cinderella's Castle is the park icon.
There are seven themed lands:
  Main Street USA, Adventureland, Frontierland, Liberty Square,
  Fantasyland, Tomorrowland, Mickey's Toontown Fair

E.P.C.O.T. opened October 1, 1982.
(Experimental Prototype Community Of Tomorrow)
This park focuses on Technology and Culture.
Spaceship Earth is the park icon.
There are two sections:
  Future World and World Showcase

Disney's Hollywood Studios opened May 1, 1989.
Originally the park was named Disney-MGM Studios and
was renamed in January 2008.
The theme is based on show business.
The Sorcerer's Hat is the park icon.
There are six themed areas:
  Hollywood Boulevard, Echo Lake, Streets of America,
  Animation Courtyard, Pixar Place, Sunset Boulevard

Animal Kingdom opened April 22, 1998.
Ihis park is aimed at animal conservation.
The Tree of Life is the park icon.
There are seven themed areas:
  The Oasis, Discovery Island, Camp Minnie-Mickey,
  Africa, Rafiki's Planet Watch, Asia, Dinoland USA

The Weenie Level

Walt Disney and his Imagineers have excelled in creating a special setting and atmosphere for the many different lands and areas throughout the parks. Each draws you into a realm of excitement, anticipation and adventure. Walt had the idea of designing and placing large elements in the parks that would create interest from a distance and draw you towards it, a "weenie" as he called it. In keeping with this theme we will look at thirty-three images of buildings, structures and elements in the parks that may have caught your attention. Have you seen...

Detail 01:

Park: _____

Area: _____

Location: _____

_____

Detail 02:

Park: _____

Area: _____

Location: _____

Detail 03:

Park: _____

Area: _____

Location: _____

_____

Detail 04:

Park: _____

Area: _____

Location: _____

_____

FEATURED DETAIL:
Did you hear that?

Detail 05:

Park: _____

Area: _____

Location: _____

_____

The research and design put into this structure is not the only Disney detail found here. If you think you hear music and dancing, do not worry because it is coming from the upper story dance and voice lesson studio as listed on the windows!

Detail 06:

Park: _____

Area: _____

Location: _____

_____

Detail 07:

Park: _____

Area: _____

Location: _____

_____

Detail 08:

Park: _____

Area: _____

Location: _____

_____

Detail 09:

Park: _____

Area: _____

Location: _____

_____

Detail 10:

Park: _____

Area: _____

Location: _____

_____

Detail 11:

Park: _____

Area: _____

Location: _____

_____

Detail 12:

Park: _____

Area: _____

Location: _____

_____

FEATURED DETAIL:
This weenie, which serves
as the park icon, is crawling
with details!

Detail 13:

Park: _____

Area: _____

Location: _____

_____

You will be overwhelmed with the amount of detail that artists have
sculpted into this park icon. With a little exploration you will be sure
to find just about every kind of animal you can think of.

Detail 14:

Park: _____

Area: _____

Location: _____

_____

Detail 15:

Park: _____

Area: _____

Location: _____

_____

Detail 16:

Park: _____

Area: _____

Location: _____

_____

Detail 17:

Park: _____

Area: _____

Location: _____

_____

Detail 18:

Park: _____

Area: _____

Location: _____

Detail 19:

Park: _____

Area: _____

Location: _____

_____

Detail 20:

Park: _____

Area: _____

Location: _____

_____

FEATURED DETAIL:
Imagineers paying attention
to the guests' line of sight.

Detail 21:

Park: _____

Area: _____

Location: _____

_____

Using this line of sight as an example, the Imagineers have thought ahead
when it comes to objects seen in the distance that might take away from
the guests' experience in the park they are currently enjoying. Notice the
color and features on the building in the back right of the image. It is not
within this park, but is actually located in an adjacent park. Refer to
the answers page for its name if you do not already know!

Detail 22:

Park: _____

Area: _____

Location: _____

_____

Detail 23:

Park: _____

Area: _____

Location: _____

_____

FEATURED DETAIL:
If you are new to the Disney Parks you may not recognize this building because it has taken a back seat to the latest park icon for this park. When this particular park opened in May of 1989 this building was a focal point for guests as they entered the main gate.

Detail 24:

Park: _____

Area: _____

Location: _____

_____

Detail 25:

Park: _____

Area: _____

Location: _____

Detail 26:

Park: _____

Area: _____

Location: _____

_____

Detail 27:

Park:

Area:

Location:

Detail 28:

Park:

Area:

Location:

Detail 29:

Park:

Area:

Location:

FEATURED DETAIL:
Once you find this relaxing spot amongst beautiful flowers and shrubs you may wonder what it is used for. Well, beyond its current use for private events, this covering of ornate metal detailing once was the loading area for a boat attraction in this park which closed due to the high maintenance cost and upkeep of the boats themselves. Refer to the answers section for the name of the attraction.

Detail 30:

Park: _____

Area: _____

Location: _____

_____

Detail 31:

Park: _____

Area: _____

Location: _____

_____

Detail 32:

Park: _____

Area: _____

Location: _____

_____

Detail 33:

Park: _____

Area: _____

Location: _____

_____

FEATURED DETAIL:

Beyond the glass windows seen here is a fairytale in itself! The restaurant inside serves breakfast, lunch and dinner and is full of character. But be sure to make your advanced dining reservations as soon as the 180 day window opens or you might only get to experience it from the perspective shown above.

First Help

The Weenie Level

The park location of each Level 1 Disney Park
Detail image is revealed in this help.

Detail 01: Disney's Hollywood Studios
Detail 02: EPCOT
Detail 03: EPCOT
Detail 04: Disney's Hollywood Studios
Detail 05: Magic Kingdom
Detail 06: Animal Kingdom
Detail 07: Disney's Hollywood Studios
Detail 08: Magic Kingdom
Detail 09: EPCOT
Detail 10: Magic Kingdom
Detail 11: Magic Kingdom
Detail 12: Animal Kingdom
Detail 13: Animal Kingdom
Detail 14: Magic Kingdom
Detail 15: Animal Kingdom
Detail 16: Animal Kingdom
Detail 17: Magic Kingdom
Detail 18: Magic Kingdom
Detail 19: Magic Kingdom
Detail 20: Disney's Hollywood Studios
Detail 21: EPCOT
Detail 22: EPCOT
Detail 23: Disney's Hollywood Studios
Detail 24: EPCOT
Detail 25: Magic Kingdom
Detail 26: EPCOT
Detail 27: Magic Kingdom
Detail 28: Disney's Hollywood Studios
Detail 29: Magic Kingdom
Detail 30: Magic Kingdom
Detail 31: EPCOT
Detail 32: EPCOT
Detail 33: Magic Kingdom

Second Help

The Weenie Level

A more general park location of each Level 1 Disney Park Detail image is revealed in this help.

Detail 01: Right down Hollywood Boulevard!

Detail 02: You can find these peaks on the west side of Future World.

Detail 03: Can't miss this as you enter EPCOT.

Detail 04: Go past Commissary Lane and take a turn down these streets.

Detail 05: Take a turn off of Main Street and you will find this facade.

Detail 06: Deep in the heart of Asia you can find these snowy peaks.

Detail 07: This ship has dropped anchor just off of Hollywood Boulevard.

Detail 08: Go to Frontierland and look for this mountain!

Detail 09: You will find this Red Planet on the east side of Future World.

Detail 10: Orbiting high above Tomorrowland is this detail.

Detail 11: This is the only mountain in Tomorrowland.

Detail 12: Check out this aged shelter in Dinoland USA.

Detail 13: This park icon is in Discovery Island.

Detail 14: Across the water from Liberty Square is this island rest area.

Detail 15: Seek refreshment at this building found in Asia.

Detail 16: Find this on the outskirts of Asia.

Detail 17: Look up in Adventureland to see this cupola detail.

Detail 18: Go to Town Square to find this Car Barn.

Detail 19: Check out this ironwork in Town Square.

Detail 20: Look beyond the Animation Courtyard.

Detail 21: Find this land in the World Showcase.

Detail 22: This can be found in the World Showcase.

Detail 23: At the end of Hollywood Boulevard near the hat.

Detail 24: Find this architecture in the World Showcase.

Detail 25: Catch a glimpse of this structure from Fantasyland.

Detail 26: Find this stone structure in the World Showcase.

Detail 27: This weather vane is found near Liberty Square.

Detail 28: Go down Sunset Boulevard to search for this structure.

Detail 29: Tasty treats await in this building in Liberty Square.

Detail 30: Find this shady spot near the Hub.

Detail 31: This temple structure is in the World Showcase.

Detail 32: This detailed replica is in the World Showcase.

Detail 33: This view can be found from Fantasyland.

The Prop Level

After being drawn into the parks, Walt and his Imagineers transport you into a world of fantasy and imagination with the proper placement of details that we will refer to as props for this level. These props set the scene and create an atmosphere for the different lands and areas throughout the parks for your enjoyment. Let us look at thirty-three more images that focus on these types of Disney details.
Have you seen...

Detail 34:

Park: _____

Area: _____

Location: _____

_____

Detail 35:

Park: _____

Area: _____

Location: _____

_____

Detail 36:

Park: _____

Area: _____

Location: _____

_____

Detail 37:

Park: _____

Area: _____

Location: _____

_____

FEATURED DETAIL:
Hold that train!

Have you ever ridden
a train at Disney?
Well, if you happen to find this one, climb
aboard! This train will take you on a short
journey to a wild place full of exploration
and learning!

Detail 38:

Park: _____

Area: _____

Location: _____

_____

25

Detail 39:

Park: _____

Area: _____

Location: _____

_____

Detail 40:

Park: _____

Area: _____

Location: _____

Detail 41:

Park: _____

Area: _____

Location: _____

_____

Detail 42:
Park: _____

Area: _____

Location: _____

_____

Detail 43:
Park: _____

Area: _____

Location: _____

Detail 44:
Park: _____

Area: _____

Location: _____

_____

27

Detail 45:

Park: _____

Area: _____

Location: _____

_____

FEATURED DETAIL:
This tree is loaded with history! Once you have found this tree seek the plaques which give insight about the tree, the hanging lanterns and the history behind it all.

Detail 46:

Park: _____

Area: _____

Location: _____

_____

?
Where

Detail 47:

Park: _____

Area: _____

Location: _____

_____

Detail 48:

Park: _____

Area: _____

Location: _____

_____

FEATURED DETAIL:
Down to the last detail! If you have ever seen these props set up in this park then you might have also taken a closer look at the actual painting. But if not, you should be paying more attention to detail! The painting is of the scene across the way.

Detail 49:

Park:

Area:

Location:

Detail 50:

Park:

Area:

Location:

Detail 51:

Park:

Area:

Location:

Detail 52:

Park: _____

Area: _____

Location: _____

_____

FEATURED DETAIL:
Imagineers follow through with their attention to detail with not only the props set on the porch in this image but also the railings, posts, light fixtures and complete building. These aesthetics truly give you a feel of a different time and place. Be sure not to breeze through town but take time to soak up your surroundings.

Detail 53:

Park: _____

Area: _____

Location: _____

_____

Detail 54:
Park: _____

Area: _____

Location: _____

_____

Detail 55:
Park: _____

Area: _____

Location: _____

Detail 56:
Park: _____

Area: _____

Location: _____

_____

Detail 57:

Park: _____

Area: _____

Location: _____

_____

Detail 58:

Park: _____

Area: _____

Location: _____

_____

FEATURED DETAIL:

Down to the shoe and nail! It is these little additions of detail that add so much depth to your experience of the parks whether you actually notice them or not. When you begin to realize these types of details it opens your eyes to another world.

This particular detail exists at a location that was used for a past attraction that is no longer in commission. Refer to the answers section for the name of the attraction.

Detail 59:

Park: _____

Area: _____

Location: _____

_____

Detail 60:

Park: _____

Area: _____

Location: _____

Detail 61:

Park: _____

Area: _____

Location: _____

_____

Detail 62:
Park: _____

Area: _____

Location: _____

_____

Detail 63:
Park: _____

Area: _____

Location: _____

_____

FEATURED DETAIL:
The addition of actual furniture, stoves, lanterns and toys with an aged look creates an accurate setting for the guests as they wander through this area of country. So next time you are sightseeing be sure to take in the all the details!

35

Detail 64:

Park: _____

Area: _____

Location: _____

_____

Detail 65:

Park: _____

Area: _____

Location: _____

Detail 66:

Park: _____

Area: _____

Location: _____

_____

First Help

The Prop Level

The park location of each Level 2 Disney Park
Detail image is revealed in this help.

Detail 34: Animal Kingdom
Detail 35: Disney's Hollywood Studios
Detail 36: Disney's Hollywood Studios
Detail 37: Magic Kingdom
Detail 38: Animal Kingdom
Detail 39: Disney's Hollywood Studios
Detail 40: Disney's Hollywood Studios
Detail 41: Animal Kingdom
Detail 42: Disney's Hollywood Studios
Detail 43: Magic Kingdom
Detail 44: Disney's Hollywood Studios
Detail 45: Magic Kingdom
Detail 46: Disney's Hollywood Studios
Detail 47: Disney's Hollywood Studios
Detail 48: EPCOT
Detail 49: Magic Kingdom
Detail 50: Disney's Hollywood Studios
Detail 51: Magic Kingdom
Detail 52: Magic Kingdom
Detail 53: Magic Kingdom
Detail 54: EPCOT
Detail 55: EPCOT
Detail 56: Disney's Hollywood Studios
Detail 57: Magic Kingdom
Detail 58: Magic Kingdom
Detail 59: Animal Kingdom
Detail 60: Magic Kingdom
Detail 61: Magic Kingdom
Detail 62: Magic Kingdom
Detail 63: EPCOT
Detail 64: Disney's Hollywood Studios
Detail 65: EPCOT
Detail 66: Magic Kingdom

Second Help

The Prop Level

A more general park location of each Level 2 Disney
Park Detail image is revealed in this help.

Detail 34: Look for these supplies in Africa.

Detail 35: Look for this crash near the Streets of America!

Detail 36: Props galore near Echo Lake.

Detail 37: Snakes! I hate snakes! Find these in Adventureland.

Detail 38: Catch this train in Africa.

Detail 39: Which way do we go from here just inside the park entrance?

Detail 40: This sign is hanging around near Echo Lake.

Detail 41: Find this direction in Dinoland USA.

Detail 42: Look in the Animation Courtyard.

Detail 43: Tomorrowland!

Detail 44: Go along Hollywood Boulevard.

Detail 45: Look in Liberty Square.

Detail 46: "C" "1" store in Pixar Place.

Detail 47: Hiding away in the Echo Lake district.

Detail 48: This artistic expression can be found in the World Showcase.

Detail 49: Between the Land of Fantasy and Tomorrow.

Detail 50: Within Echo Lake.

Detail 51: Search through Fantasyland.

Detail 52: Down in Frontierland.

Detail 53: Look closely in Frontierland.

Detail 54: World Showcase hides this water well.

Detail 55: The World Showcase holds this timepiece.

Detail 56: Rats in the Streets of America!

Detail 57: Look out for this detail in Frontierland.

Detail 58: Good luck finding this detail in Liberty Square.

Detail 59: Look along this Trek in Asia.

Detail 60: A sign that you are entering Adventureland!

Detail 61: Take notice of this planter in Adventureland.

Detail 62: Off the beaten path of the Hub.

Detail 63: The World Showcase harbors these props.

Detail 64: Look for this snow on the Streets of America!

Detail 65: Look for this booth in the World Showcase.

Detail 66: Wait here while I go look in the Briar Patch.

The Pixie Dust Level

Finally, you have been drawn in and immersed into the world of fantasy and imagination that Walt and his Imagineers have created for you only to discover that the attention to detail goes even further. If you take the time to explore, you may be surprised to find that little extra pixie dust detail which continues the story line and adds to your enjoyment of the parks. These final thirty-three images focus on special details that you may never see unless you begin to pay attention to detail! Have you seen...

Detail 67:

Park: _____

Area: _____

Location: _____

_____

FEATURED DETAIL:
Everything may not be what it seems at Walt Disney World! Take this trash can for example. It is a mobile and vocal trash can that will draw kids like flies. This detail can be found in a certain area of this park and if you have ever seen it, you know there is always a crowd.

Detail 68:

Park: _____

Area: _____

Location: _____

_____

Detail 69:

Park: _____

Area: _____

Location: _____

_____

Detail 70:

Park: _____

Area: _____

Location: _____

_____

FEATURED DETAIL:

Mine!....Mine! Mine!........Mine!

Imagineers take a simple entrance area and bring life to it, adding to every guest's enjoyment. This detail will bring a smile to your face if you have seen the popular animated movie from which these birds came........Mine!

Where

Disney Park Details (Level 3)

Have you ever noticed the ground on which you walk in the parks?

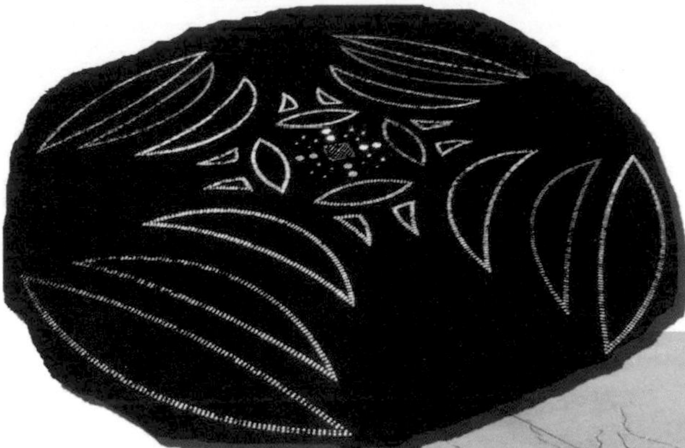

Detail 71:

Park: ____________________

Area: ____________________

Location: ____________________

____

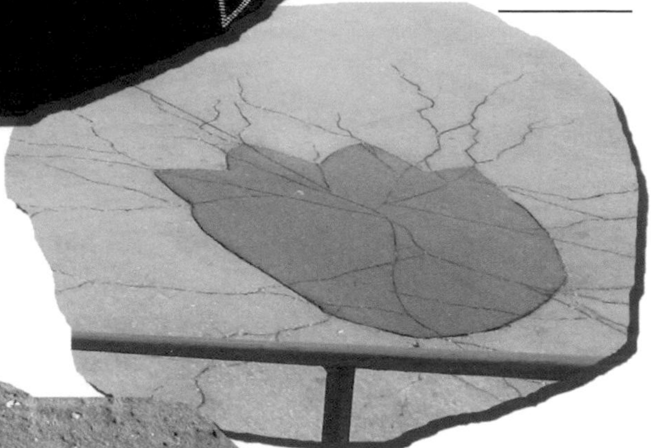

Detail 72:

Park: ____________________

Area: ____________________

Location: ____________________

____

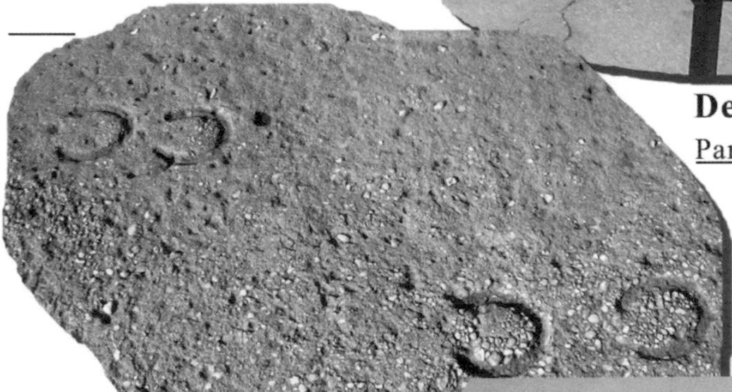

Detail 73:

Park: ____________________

Area: ____________________

Location: ____________________

____

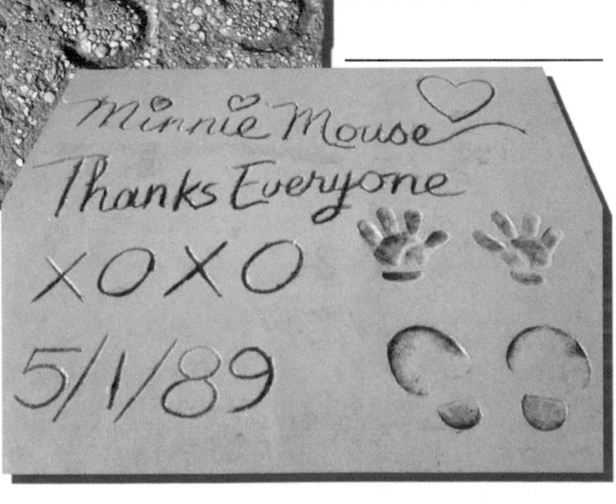

Detail 74:

Park: ____________________

Area: ____________________

Location: ____________________

____

Disney Park Details (Level 3)

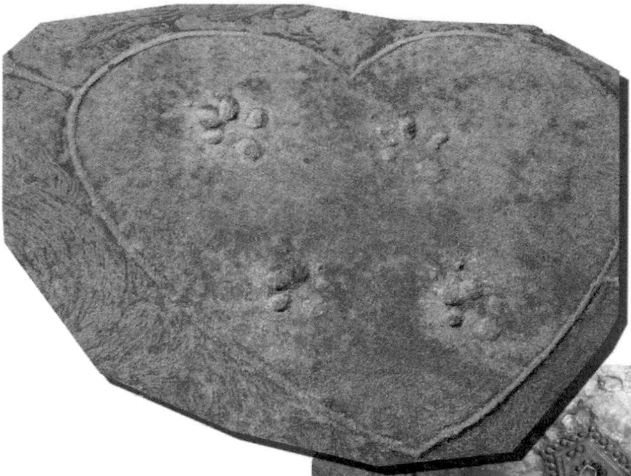

Detail 75:

Park: ____________________

Area: ____________________

Location: ____________________

____

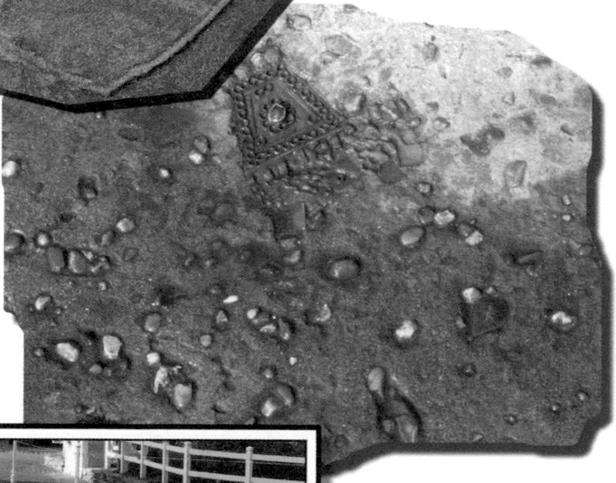

Detail 76:

Park: ____________________

Area: ____________________

Location: ____________________

____

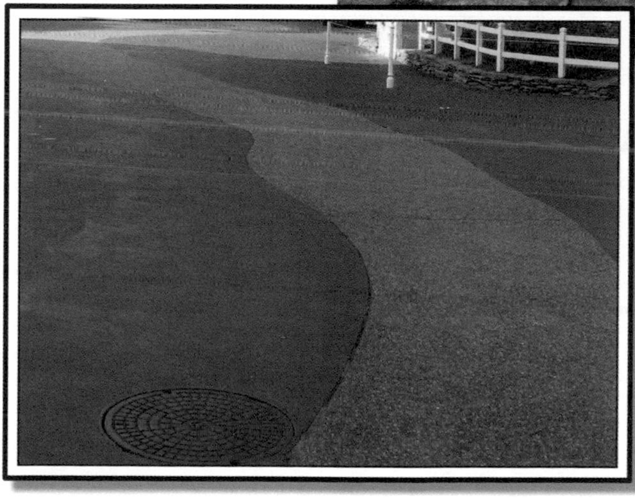

Detail 77:

Park: ____________________

Area: ____________________

Location: ____________________

____

Next time you are in this area, see if you can find a cast member who can tell you the reason behind this pavement flow!

Detail 78:

Park: _____

Area: _____

Location: _____

_____

Detail 79:

Park: _____

Area: _____

Location: _____

_____

Detail 80:

Park: _____

Area: _____

Location: _____

_____

Detail 81:

Park: _____

Area: _____

Location: _____

_____

Detail 82:

Park: _____

Area: _____

Location: _____

_____

Detail 83:

Park: _____

Area: _____

Location: _____

_____

FEATURED DETAIL:
Have you seen this statue of Cinderella and her little friends?

Detail 84:

Park: _____

Area: _____

Location: _____

_____

An added detail to this statue is a continuation of the storyline: If you lean down just enough you can see Cinderella being crowned. This photo shows the proper angle which aligns the statue with the crown on the backdrop which alludes to her future royalty!

Detail 85:

Park: _____

Area: _____

Location: _____

_____

Murals
located throughout the Walt Disney World Parks
continue or add to the storylines of their particular area.
Take time to look at the design and detail put into each of these
works of art.

Detail 86:

Park: _____

Area: _____

Location: _____

_____

Detail 87:

Park: _____

Area: _____

Location: _____

_____

Detail 88:

Park: _____

Area: _____

Location: _____

_____

Detail 89:

Park: _____

Area: _____

Location: _____

Detail 90:

Park: _____

Area: _____

Location: _____

_____

Detail 91:
Park: _____

Area: _____

Location: _____

_____

FEATURED DETAIL:
I wonder where that beanstalk goes.
Explore the shop at this location and you will find more details to this tale, including a character who has a giant part in the story!

Detail 92:
Park: _____

Area: _____

Location: _____

_____

FEATURED DETAIL:
This Barber Shop is not just a fitting facade for this area but an actual working shop that anyone can stop in and get a cut.

Detail 93:

Park: _____

Area: _____

Location: _____

_____

FEATURED DETAIL:
This peaceful water way
creates a separation between
two areas of this park as well
as symbolizes a river that
similarly separates areas of
this country!

Detail 94:

Park: _____

Area: _____

Location: _____

_____

Remembrance
There are many details in the parks that give recognition
to those who have contributed to this amazing place.

Detail 95:

Park: _____

Area: _____

Location: _____

_____

Detail 96:

Park: _____

Area: _____

Location: _____

_____

Detail 97:

Park: _____

Area: _____

Location: _____

_____

53

Detail 98:

Park:_____

Area:_____

Location:_____

_____

FEATURED DETAIL:
Even with the great detail that Imagineers have already put into the parks they continue to amaze guests with park overlays during holiday seasons. Check out the ice over of this popular park icon!

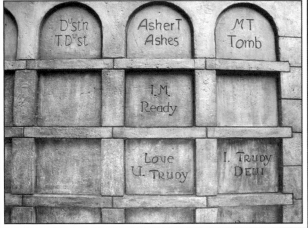

Detail 99:

Park:_____

Area:_____

Location:_____

_____

As we close out this book on the Walt Disney World parks we leave you with an image of a detail that is just inside the perimeter of this attraction.

Imagineers have added details to the attractions which add to the guest's enjoyment if they pay attention to detail! Look for our book that focuses on Disney attraction details that will be available soon.

First Help

The Pixie Dust Level

The park location of each Level 3 Disney Park
Detail image is revealed in this help.

Detail 67: Magic Kingdom Park
Detail 68: Disney's Hollywood Studios
Detail 69: Magic Kingdom
Detail 70: EPCOT
Detail 71: EPCOT
Detail 72: Disney's Hollywood Studios
Detail 73: Magic Kingdom
Detail 74: Disney's Hollywood Studios
Detail 75: Magic Kingdom
Detail 76: Magic Kingdom
Detail 77: Magic Kingdom
Detail 78: EPCOT
Detail 79: Magic Kingdom
Detail 80: Animal Kingdom
Detail 81: EPCOT
Detail 82: Magic Kingdom
Detail 83: Animal Kingdom
Detail 84: Magic Kingdom
Detail 85: Disney's Hollywood Studios
Detail 86: Magic Kingdom
Detail 87: EPCOT
Detail 88: Magic Kingdom
Detail 89: Disney's Hollywood Studios
Detail 90: Disney's Hollywood Studios
Detail 91: Magic Kingdom
Detail 92: Magic Kingdom
Detail 93: EPCOT
Detail 94: Magic Kingdom
Detail 95: Magic Kingdom
Detail 96: Disney's Hollywood Studios
Detail 97: Magic Kingdom
Detail 98: Magic Kingdom
Detail 99: Magic Kingdom

Second Help

The Pixie Dust Level

A more general park location of each Level 3 Disney
Park Detail image is revealed in this help.

Detail 67: Search the trash cans in Tomorrowland.

Detail 68: Look around Echo Lake for this detail.

Detail 69: Inside one of the shops on Main Street is this phone.

Detail 70: Listen for "MINE" on the west side of Future World.

Detail 71: Check out this pavement in Future World.

Detail 72: These prints are around Echo Lake.

Detail 73: Find these horseshoe prints in Liberty Square.

Detail 74: Look down Hollywood Boulevard for this walk of fame.

Detail 75: Take a close look around the Town Square.

Detail 76: Search for this treasure in Adventureland.

Detail 77: It's running through Liberty Square.

Detail 78: Search out World Showcase for this background.

Detail 79: Near the Hub lurks this topiary monster!

Detail 80: Focus on Rafiki's Planet Watch.

Detail 81: Check out this building detail in the World Showcase.

Detail 82: Look around the Hub for this detail.

Detail 83: Colorful Buildings! Look in Dinoland USA.

Detail 84: Look around Fantasyland.

Detail 85: Look in the back of the Streets of America area.

Detail 86: Search the castle for this mural.

Detail 87: Look to the west side of Future World for this mural.

Detail 88: Look in Tomorrowland for this Robo Newz.

Detail 89: This FX detail is near the Streets of America.

Detail 90: Search around the Streets of America.

Detail 91: Look around Fantasyland.

Detail 92: Look for the barber pole in Town Square.

Detail 93: This upward waterfall fits this area in Future World.

Detail 94: Search between Liberty Square and Frontierland.

Detail 95: Look up, down the Main Street area.

Detail 96: Off of Echo Lake is this famed area.

Detail 97: Look around Town Square.

Detail 98: During Christmas is when the lights on this icon are visible.

Detail 99: Look just inside this attraction area near Liberty Square.

ANSWERS

The following pages contain answers to the Disney Park Details contained in this book along with additional information and tidbits! So, if you have used all your helps and still do not know where you can find the image or just want to make sure you were correct, go ahead and take a look!

ANSWERS

Detail 01: This is the Sorcerer's Hat located at the end of Hollywood Boulevard in Disney's Hollywood Studios. It serves as the park icon and main weenie which draws guests to the central crossroads of the park. This hat was inspired by the Disney animated film The Sorcerer's Apprentice and replaced the previous park icon, the Earful Tower, in 2001. It also hides the original park weenie, the Grauman's Chinese Theater.

Detail 02: This is the glass mountain range of the Imagination Pavilion found on the west side of Future World in EPCOT and home to the Journey Into Imagination With Figment Attraction.

Detail 03: This is Spaceship Earth, the "Big Golf Ball" as some call it, located at the entrance in EPCOT. This park icon is a complete geodesic sphere reaching eighteen stories in height and containing an attraction by the same name inside.

Detail 04: This is a row of residence facades on Gillespie Street in the Streets of America area in Disney's Hollywood Studios. They are located behind Commissary Lane toward the back of the park. If you are ever down this alley at Christmas time you can see the incredible lighting effects of the Osborne Lights. It has also been said that if you listen closely you can even hear the sounds of busy city streets.

Detail 05: This is a building facade located on Center Street, just off of Main Street in Magic Kingdom. If you look closely at the upper story windows you will see references to a dance & voice lesson studio. From this location you can hear sounds of classes taking place, if the park noise is not too loud.

Detail 06: These are the snowy peaks of the Expedition Everest Attraction in the land of Asia in Animal Kingdom. Imagineers put in many hours of research to bring this attraction to life. During the ride you cross over the tallest peak known as the Forbidden Mountain in an effort to get to Mount Everest (marked by the arrow in

the adjacent image) only to run into some problems along the way!

Detail 07: This is the S.S. Down the Hatch found at the edge of Echo Lake closest to the Sorcerer's Hat in Disney's Hollywood Studios. It serves as a snack location for the main hub of the park.

Detail 08: This is the pinacle of the Splash Mountain Attraction in Frontierland in Magic Kingdom. This is a log ride attraction based on the story of Brer Rabbit of the animated Disney classic Song of the South.

Detail 09: This is a close up of the Red Planet at the entrance of the Mission: Space Attraction found on the east side of Future World in EPCOT. This attraction opened in 2003 replacing the former Horizons pavilion.

Detail 10: This is a glimpse of the orbiting planets of the Astro Orbiter Attraction in Tomorrowland in Magic Kingdom. This rocket ride is atop Rocket Tower Plaza and is accessed via an elevator found on the side of the plaza closest to the Space Mountain Attraction. This planetary sculpture takes on a whole new feel at night with its illumination!

Detail 11: This is the well known futuristic peak of the Space Mountain Attraction in Tomorrowland in Magic Kingdom. As guests approach the park, the view of this building causes a sense of anticipation of the fun that awaits!

Detail 12: This is a building extension of Restaurantasaurus in Dinoland USA in Animal Kingdom. It takes the form of an old rusted barrack apparently used by paleontologists while digging for dinosaur bones.

Detail 13: This is the Tree Of Life, located in the center of Discovery Island in Animal Kingdom. It is covered with over 320 animal carvings by twenty different artists. Next time you visit this park take the time to explore the wonderful detail found all around the trunk of this tree. This park icon also serves as the home of the It's Tough to be a Bug Attraction, a Disney 4-D show not to be missed!

Detail 14: This is Aunt Polly's Dockside Inn located on Tom Sawyer's Island in Frontierland in Magic Kingdom. This shady spot, as seen from the Liberty Belle Riverboat Dock in Liberty Square, used to serve picnic lunches that you could enjoy in this peaceful setting.

Detail 15: This is a refreshment building found on your left as you cross the bridge from Asia to Discovery Island in Animal Kingdom.

Detail 16: This covered area and dock are located in Asia across from the Flights of Wonder Theatre in Animal Kingdom. It served as one of the loading areas for the Discovery River Boats Attraction (which only stayed in operation about a year after the park opened in 1998).

Detail 17: This is the cupola detail found atop the Zanzibar Trading Company Shop in Adventureland in Magic Kingdom across from the Swiss Family Treehouse Attraction.

Detail 18: This is the Car Barn found in Town Square between the Firehouse and Barber Shop in Magic Kingdom. It is the starting point for the Main Street Vehicles and parades.

Detail 19: This is the park side view of the Train Station in Town Square in Magic Kingdom showing the ironwork detail.

Detail 20: This is the Earful Tower, the original park icon for Disney's Hollywood Studios, located on the outskirts of the park behind the buildings in the Animation Courtyard. This 130 foot tall water tower is not a working water tower but was built to add to the characteristics of the studios of old.

Detail 21: This is the Morocco Pavilion in World Showcase in EPCOT as seen from Future World. The building just to the right (marked with the arrow in the adjacent picture) is the Tower of Terror Attraction in Disney's Hollywood Studios. Imagineers blended the look of this attraction

with Morocco by adding architectural features, such as spires, and using similar color tones so as not to distract from the view of the guests. This technique is used throughout the parks.

Detail 22: This is the entryway to the China Pavilion in World Showcase in EPCOT. The amount of detail shown on the entry is carried throughout this pavilion.

Detail 23: This is a scaled replica of the famous Grauman's Chinese Theatre facade in Hollywood, California and is found behind the Sorcerer's Hat on Hollywood Boulevard in Disney's Hollywood Studios. This building served as the original weenie for the park as guests entered.

Detail 24: This is a grouping of buildings on the left side of the Germany Pavilion in World Showcase in EPCOT.

Detail 25: This ornate structure is the old Skyway Station on the hilltop of Fantasyland in Magic Kingdom. It transported guests back and forth to Tomorrowland by gondola lift vehicles. This attraction opened with the park in 1971 and was closed in late 1999.

Detail 26: This is the beautiful stone work of the Akershus Royal Banquet Hall found on the right side of the Norway Pavilion in World Showcase in EPCOT. Within these walls is home to the Princess Storybook Character Dining.

Detail 27: This is the cupola with bat weather vane on the Haunted Mansion in Liberty Square in Magic Kingdom. This place is crawling with spooky details so keep your eyes open while heading through the grounds of this original park attraction!

Detail 28: This is a different angle of the Tower of Terror Attraction at the end of Sunset Boulevard in Disney's Hollywood Studios.

Detail 29: This is the Sleepy Hollow refreshment area on the right just as you enter into Liberty Square in Magic Kingdom. Excellent treats are ready to be had here!

Detail 30:   This was the loading area for the Plaza Swan Boats Attraction located just to the right of the hub in Magic Kingdom. It was a picturesque attraction as swan shaped boats glided around the castle moat and through the beautiful grounds. This attraction closed in 1983. The loading area is used as a covering for special events.

Detail 31: This is the step pyramid at the Mexico Pavilion in World Showcase in EPCOT which contains a restaurant, attraction and shopping for your enjoyment all under a star filled evening sky!

Detail 32: This is a replica of Venice's Doge's Palace at the Italy Pavilion in World Showcase in EPCOT. Imagineers draw guests into the pavilion with the beauty of the materials and attention to the detail of the design.

Detail 33: This is Cinderella's Castle as seen from Fantasyland in Magic Kingdom. Within these decorative castle windows you will find Cinderella's Royal Table Restaurant. It serves character meals throughout the day for all little prince and princesses to enjoy.

Detail 34: This is a set of supplies parked along the wall of the river bank near the bridge in Africa before crossing over to Discovery Island in Animal Kingdom.

Detail 35: This is a crash scene at the entrance of the Studio Backlot Tour Attraction back in the Streets of America area in Disney's Hollywood Studios.

Detail 36: This is an arrangement of props in front of the Indiana Jones Epic Stunt Spectacular Attraction in the Echo Lake area in Disney's Hollywood Studios.

Detail 37: This is a snake cart display found outside the entrance to the Zanzibar Trading Company shop near the Magic Carpets of Aladdin Attraction in Adventureland in Magic Kingdom.

Detail 38: This is the Wildlife Express Train which can be caught in Africa in Animal Kingdom near the Pangani Forest Exploration Trail. It transports you to Rafiki's Planet Watch and Conservation Station.

Detail 39: This is a directional sign next to Sid Cahuenga's One-of-a-Kind Shop which is on the left of the entry plaza as you enter Disney's Hollywood Studios.

Detail 40: This is the Tune In Lounge sign which is next to the 50's Prime Time Cafe in the Echo Lake area in Disney's Hollywood Studios. The neon sign and building architecture in this area transport guests back to the 50's and 60's.

Detail 41: This is an early version travel trailer parked next to Restaurantosaurus in Dinoland USA in Animal Kingdom.

Detail 42: This is a sign to the Magic of Disney Animation Attraction in the Animation Courtyard in Disney's Hollywood Studios. Notice the tools of the trade that make up this sign: paint brush, pencil and film strip.

Detail 43: This is additional signage for Stitch's Great Escape in Tomorrowland in Magic Kingdom. The futuristic detailing of the signage and the metallic materials used in its construction transport guests into an alien environment!

Detail 44: This is a traffic light on Hollywood Boulevard in Disney's Hollywood Studios which adds to the feel of an earlier era and setting.

Detail 45: This is the Liberty Tree, an actual 100 year old tree, located in Liberty Square in Magic Kingdom. This tree was found on the original property of Walt Disney World and was transplanted to its current location during the park's construction. The lanterns that hang in the tree represent the original thirteen colonies. Additional information about the Liberty Tree can be found on a plaque near the tree.

Detail 46: This is a battleship board ceiling in the shop across from the Toy Story Midway Mania Attraction in Pixar Place in Disney's Hollywood Studios. This whole area of the park is a wonderful flashback to the toys and games we all loved to play as kids!

Detail 47: This is the Echo Lake Apartments entry gate right next to the 50's Prime Time Cafe Restaurant in Disney's Hollywood Studios. Imagineers disguise non guest areas such as this gate so as not to bring an abrupt stop to the theme of that area.

Detail 48: This is a display of props just before you enter the France Pavilion in World Showcase in EPCOT. Look down to the right along the ledge as you cross over the last bridge into France from the United Kingdom. Take a close look at the painting on the easel and see if you recognize the scene which is across the way.

Detail 49: This lantern and stonework is at the Fairytale Garden Theatre which is hidden to the right of the castle between Fantasyland and Tomorrowland in Magic Kingdom. It is across from Cosmic Ray's Starlight Cafe and features Storytime with Belle as she tells her story about a Beast!

Detail 50: This is Gertie the Dinosaur found at the edge of Echo Lake near the Indiana Jones Epic Stunt Spectacular Attraction entrance in Disney's Hollywood Studios. This dinosaur is an example of programmatic architecture: the use of the dinosaur form as a building for a soft serve ice cream stand.

It has also been said that this dinosaur is a reference to the 1914 American animated short, Gertie the Dinosaur, by Winsor McCay. This film set a standard that would be later carried on by Walt Disney and other animators by giving character to an animated animal.

Detail 51: This tree was the centerpiece for Pooh's Playful Spot in Fantasyland in Magic Kingdom from 2005 - 2010. The tree has been moved to the entrance of the Many Adventures of Winnie the Pooh Attraction due to a major Fantasyland expansion that has removed this playground.

Detail 52: This is the General Store near the Country Bear Jamboree Attraction in Frontierland in Magic Kingdom. It is covered in period details from the millwork on the porch, to the horse rail out front to tie off your ride as you come into town!

Detail 53: This is the facade of Brer Rabbit's house at the Briar Patch store located in the side of the Splash Mountain Attraction in Frontierland in Magic Kingdom.

Detail 54: This is Snow White's wishing well found on the left side of the Germany Pavilion in World Showcase in EPCOT. The best known version of this fairy tale came from Germany and so it seems the proper setting for this detail.

Detail 55: This clock is a centerpiece on the central tower facade of the Biergarten Restaurant in the Germany Pavilion in World Showcase in EPCOT.

Detail 56: These are the rats from the fountain near the entrance to the Muppet Vision 3-D Attraction in the Streets of America area in Disney's Hollywood Studios filling their boat with loot. Take a closer look at the rat in the front of the boat fishing for the coins thrown into the fountain by guests!

Detail 57: This is a tower fort along the edge of the Rivers of America near the Country Bear Jamboree Attraction in Frontierland in Magic Kingdom.

Detail 58: These are the horse shoes hanging on the structure of a past attraction loading area, known as the Mike Fink Keel Boats, at the edge of the Rivers of America in the Liberty Square area in Magic Kingdom. This boat ride attraction was based on Disney television shows and movies that featured Davy Crockett and it opened with the park in 1971. After problems arose with the boats, this attraction closed in 1997 and the loading area is now used primarily for stroller parking.

Detail 59: This detail is along the Maharajah Jungle Trek at the Bat Cliffs in Asia in Animal Kingdom. Imagineers have done their homework again with the props and details surrounding the guests so they become immersed into this setting.

Detail 60: This spear and shield prop is on the railing of the bridge leading into Adventureland in Magic Kingdom.

Detail 61: This planter is found in front of the Jungle Cruise Attraction area in Adventureland in Magic Kingdom. Imagineers make a planter out of what looks like a wooden cargo box with faded stencil lettering of an exotic plant company. This adds to the attraction itself and the theme of the surrounding land.

Detail 62: This lamp post is found at the crossover from the bridge entrance of Adventureland to Liberty Square in Magic Kingdom. Imagineers give a foreshadowing of the area ahead with the colonial style materials and construction used for this light pole.

Detail 63: This Kidcot Fun Stop station is at the American Pavilion in World Showcase in EPCOT and is decked out in details from the colonial period. These Kidcot stations are located throughout EPCOT and provide a nice break for children as they decorate a keepsake.

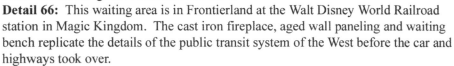

Detail 64: This snowman is located just down from the Toy Story Pizza Planet Arcade in the Streets of America area in Disney's Hollywood Studios.

Detail 65: This easy to spot telephone booth is located in the United Kingdom Pavilion in EPCOT.

Detail 66: This waiting area is in Frontierland at the Walt Disney World Railroad station in Magic Kingdom. The cast iron fireplace, aged wall paneling and waiting bench replicate the details of the public transit system of the West before the car and highways took over.

Detail 67: This is Push, the talking trash can and radio controlled robot that interacts with guests in the Tomorrowland area in Magic Kingdom. Usually surrounded by children trying to figure out how it works, Push is a regular steel lined trash can with a plastic bag insert that hides the robotic system and transmitter. Other interactive robots like Push include Wes Palm, a talking Palm Tree, and Pipa, another talking trash can, located in Animal Kingdom.

Detail 68: "Warning Do Not Pull Rope" - Yes the Imagineers DO want you to pull this rope at the well located to the left of the Indiana Jones Epic Stunt Spectacular Attraction in the Echo Lake area in Disney's Hollywood Studios. So next time you walk past this detail do pull and see what happens!

Detail 69: This is the Gossip phone located in the Chapeau Shop off of Main Street USA in Magic Kingdom. Search the store and once you find it, pick it up to hear the latest gossip!

Detail 70: This is the flock of seagulls at the entrance area of the Living Seas Pavilion on the west side of Future World in EPCOT. Imagineers bring life to this entrance area with the insisting chatter of "Mine, Mine, Mine!" that these birds are famous for in the 2003 animated hit Finding Nemo.

Detail 71: This is one of the fiberoptic paving panels on the walkway area between Innoventions and Spaceship Earth in EPCOT. It is an amazing detail of color and surprise as guests walk along this path in Future World at night.

Detail 72: These are the dinosaur foot prints at the Echo Lake area in Disney's Hollywood Studios. They cross the pavement into the grass and lead guests right to the culprit, Gertie the Dinosaur!

Detail 73: These are the horseshoe imprints in the pavement just inside the exit area of the Haunted Mansion Attraction in Liberty Square in Magic Kingdom. These prints must belong to the ghost horse harnessed to the black hearse nearby.

Detail 74: This is Minnie Mouse's signature and prints found with others just inside the courtyard of the Grauman's Chinese Theatre behind the Sorcerer's Hat on Hollywood Boulevard in Disney's Hollywood Studios. There are more prints to see in this Disney version walk of fame!

Detail 75: This heart is on the sidewalk in front of Tony's Town Square Restaurant in Town Square in Magic Kingdom. This Italian restaurant is themed after the 1955 animated film Lady and the Tramp. As you can see the theme flows out onto the sidewalk. Be sure to check out the details inside!

Detail 76: This is the gem filled pavement around the Magic Carpets of Aladdin Attraction in Adventureland in Magic Kingdom. Don't get too greedy because these gems are not real but a worthy aggregate to continue the theme for this area.

Detail 77: This odd pattern of paving is found throughout Liberty Square in Magic Kingdom and it definitely raises one's curiosity if noticed. So next time you are in the area see if you can find out why it is there!

Detail 78: This is a wall of sea monsters placed to the left of the Norway Pavilion in World Showcase in EPCOT. These creatures are often mentioned in that country's ancient lore of sea exploration.

Detail 79: This topiary serpent can be found down by the water just to the right of the hub towards Tomorrowland in Magic Kingdom. Take a close look at the shrubbery throughout the parks as they resemble different characters and creatures in this green thumb art form!

Detail 80: This bug is part of a bigger picture, one of conservation, at the entrance to Animal Kingdom's Conservation Station at Rafiki's Planet Watch. This is the facade that greets guests when they enter the building.

Detail 81: This is just one of the many architectural details found throughout the Walt Disney World Parks. This particular detail is the cornice work found along the parapet of the Morocco Pavilion in World Showcase in EPCOT.

Detail 82: This uniquely detailed post is found at the Hub in Magic Kingdom and shows that Walt and his Imagineers look into all details concerning their designs. This tradition continues today as the parks transform and expand.

Detail 83: This very playful section of buildings is in Dinoland USA in Animal Kingdom. Along with the vibrant colors are the building details which take on the characteristics of various animals.

Detail 84: This is the fountain statue of Cinderella and her friends found just to the left of the castle as you exit the tunnel into Fantasyland in Magic Kingdom. Notice how Cinderella is dressed in her peasant clothes and the crown on the background is alluding to her future as a princess. This is an exceptional detail that adds to the enjoyment of the guests' experience when they notice this correlation.

Detail 85: This is the mermaid fountain that was used in the 1984 hit movie <u>Splash</u> and can be found near the entrance to the Studio Backlot Tour Attraction in the Streets of America area in Disney's Hollywood Studios.

Detail 86: This beautiful mural is located inside the tunnel of Cinderella's Castle in Magic Kingdom. This and adjacent murals show the story of Cinderella as guests pass from the hub into Fantasyland.

Detail 87: This mural is found along the entry walls to the Land Pavilion on the west side of Future World in EPCOT.

Detail 88: This Robo Newz stand is found near the entrance to the TTA (Tomorrowland Transit Authority) in Tomorrowland in Magic Kingdom. Imagineers continue the galactic theme and storyline of this futuristic land with a look at what the news boy will evolve into.

Detail 89: This is the effects generator next to the Muppet Vision 3-D Attraction in the Streets of America in Disney's Hollywood Studios. Imagineers have a little fun with this Muppet themed area.

Detail 90: These pipes are located on the back side of the Muppet Vision 3-D Attraction in the Streets of America in Disney's Hollywood Studios.

Imagineers have taken this opportunity to add even more detail to their story by adding some colorful painting and symbols to this typical building system located in an area that most guests walk right by without noticing.

Detail 91: This beanstalk is outside of the Sir Mickey's gift shop located in Fantasyland, just behind the castle, in Magic Kingdom. This shop is themed with details from the Mickey and the Beanstalk segment of the animated film <u>Fun and Fancy Free,</u> that was originally released to theatres in 1947. Be sure to look in this shop for a giant detail!

Detail 92: This is the Barber Shop found on the left side of Town Square, between the Emporium and Car Barn, as you enter into Magic Kingdom.

Detail 93: This is the backward waterfall which fits in perfectly with the Imagination Pavilion on the west side of Future World in EPCOT.

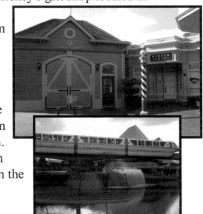

Detail 94: This river detail is found between Liberty Square and Frontierland in Magic Kingdom and runs from a silver plate out into the Rivers of America. This detail creates a transition between the two lands and their architecture. Furthermore, it represents the Mississippi River which separates the Colonial style of the East coast from the booming growth of the frontier to the West.

Detail 95: This is Walt's window located above the Plaza Ice Cream Palor on Main Street USA facing the castle in Magic Kingdom. The reason given for this location was that Walt loved ice cream and the window overlooked his beloved castle. Imagineers have used the windows on Main Street to comemorate many people who had a part in the making of this park. Next time you walk down Main Street, take a look at the unique way that people are remembered!

Detail 96: This is the Academy of Television Arts & Sciences Hall of Fame located to the left of the American Idol Experience Attraction in the Echo Lake area in Disney's Hollywood Studios. It contains busts of famous entertainers including Walt Disney himself.

Detail 97: This is the statue of Roy O. Disney sitting on a park bench with Minnie Mouse which is found in the central courtyard of Town Square in Magic Kingdom. After Walt Disney's untimely death, his brother Roy watched over the construction of Disney World in Orlando, Florida. At its completion, Roy renamed the park, "Walt Disney World," as a tribute to his brother.

Detail 98: This is Cinderella's Castle in Magic Kingdom. It is adorned with glimmering icicle lights which can be seen during the Christmas holidays and is a breathtaking sight in the night sky! Imagineers transform the castle for different holidays and celebrations, but this ice overlay has to be among the most dazzling!

Detail 99: This is a wall of tombs found in the exit area of the Haunted Mansion Attraction in Liberty Square in Magic Kingdom. Imagineers add some comic relief to this morbid setting with a play on words.

There are many of these details throughout the attractions at the Walt Disney World Parks and each add additional enjoyment to the guest's experience. If you have enjoyed this Attention to Detail compilation, please keep your eyes peeled for our book which focuses on attractions.

Disney Detail Park Breakdown

For your convenience, we have gathered the Disney Details in this book with the park that you can find them in.

Magic Kingdom Park:
05, 08, 10, 11, 14, 17, 18, 19, 25, 27, 29, 30, 33, 37, 43, 45, 49, 51, 52, 53, 57, 58, 60, 61, 62, 66, 67, 69, 73, 75, 76, 77, 79, 82, 84, 86, 88, 91, 92, 94, 95, 97, 98, 99

Animal Kingdom Park:
06, 12, 13, 15, 16, 34, 38, 41, 59, 80, 83

EPCOT:
02, 03, 09, 21, 22, 24, 26, 31, 32, 48, 54, 55, 63, 65, 70, 71, 78, 81, 87, 93

Disney's Hollywood Studios:
01, 04, 07, 20, 23, 28, 35, 36, 39, 40, 42, 44, 46, 47, 50, 56, 64, 68, 72, 74, 85, 89, 90, 96

Walt Disney was always looking at his parks and thinking about ways to improve them. With that in mind it must be noted that as the parks evolve, change and update some of the details shown in this book may change or even disappear.

Commission:

Now that you have seen these 99 images, there is always room for one more!
We hope this book has opened your eyes to view what Walt Disney and his Imagineers have created for each of us to encounter and enjoy at the Walt Disney World Parks in Orlando, Florida.
So in future visits we hope you will pay
Attention To Detail.

Attention to Detail
Magic Kingdom Hunt

Object:
To seek, find, and capture a picture of as many of the twelve details contained in this Magic Kingdom Hunt within the time limit set.

Time Limit:
90 minutes

Rules:
1) Group into teams with each team having a camera device.
2) Select a location to meet at when the time expires.
3) One member must take a picture of the other team members with the detail. The same person does not have to always take the pictures but all other team members must be in the picture.
4) Gather together to see which team was able to seek, find and capture the most Disney Details with their team.

Reminder:
Don't forget to make a copy of this hunt for each team if they do not have their own book. Also, be careful not to interfere or disturb other guests at the park while you engage in the scavenger hunt.

Variations:
- You can vary the time limit to fit your schedule or just hunt throughout the day.
- You can hunt by yourself or with teams.
- You can prepare ahead in finding the images or not look at them until the hunt starts.
- Turn on the date/time stamp on your cameras to see who took the pictures the fastest or within the time limit.

Turn the page to get started

12 Magic Kingdom Details await

Seek, Find and Click!

MK001.1   - Tomorrowland
MK001.2   - Fantasyland
MK001.3   - Adventureland
MK001.4   - Frontierland
MK001.5   - Main Street
MK001.6   - Fantasyland
MK001.7   - Adventureland
MK001.8   - Hub
MK001.9   - Frontierland
MK001.10 - Main Street
MK001.11 - Tomorrowland
MK001.12 - Town Square

Scavenger Hunt 001

Object:
Using the thirty-three phrases below take a picture of what Disney detail comes to your mind while in the parks. You can do this in groups or by yourself; in a set amount of time or during the length of your trip. The main rule is to just have fun and be creative!

1 - show a little character
2 - tea for two
3 - lots of spots
4 - street of dreams
5 - hats off to you
6 - that's just goofy!
7 - be our guest
8 - give a little whistle
9 - beautiful tomorrow
10 - it will come around
11 - draw me close
12 - what time is it?
13 - ready, set, go!
14 - tools of the trade
15 - mirror, mirror, on the wall
16 - not my size
17 - rain, rain, go away
18 - how do you do?
19 - make a wish!
20 - perfect fit
21 - I'm stuffed
22 - are you "fur" real?
23 - true blue
24 - under the sea
25 - what's your point?
26 - let's roll
27 - one bad apple
28 - green with envy
29 - that will leave a mark
30 - what's that smell?
31 - it's over my head
32 - pretty in pink
33 - dreams come true

About the Authors

Keith Black ~ Author/Graphics

Keith Black became introduced to the world of Disney after visiting Walt Disney World with his wife and two young daughters back in 2003. He quickly realized the wonderful family environment the resort offered and has taken his family back each year. With his background in architecture and engineering Keith has been intrigued with the life's work of Walt Disney and his Imagineers.

Favorite Park: Magic Kingdom
Favorite Time to visit: Fall
Favorite Details:
    Level 1:   Detail 10
    Level 2:   Detail 42
    Level 3:   Detail 84

Jacquelyn Damon ~ CoAuthor/Photographer

Jackie Damon is a veteran visitor to Walt Disney World. During her first visit in 1973 her love for the Disney Parks began and continued to grow to include everything at this special place. Jackie has always had a great interest in photography and enjoys capturing the many unique details all around Walt Disney World to share with others.

Favorite Park: Magic Kingdom
Favorite Time to visit: Winter
Favorite Details:
    Level 1:   Detail 33
    Level 2:   Detail 51
    Level 3:   Detail 95

Made in the USA
Lexington, KY
27 November 2010